On Computer Simulated Universes

Mark J. Solomon

Lithp Preth Publishing • *Hillsborough, NC* • 2013

Printed in the United States of America

First Printing (1.0), August 2013

ISBN 978-0-9898325-1-9

Lithp Preth Publishing
110 East Queen Street
Hillsborough, NC 27278

LithpPreth.com
Editor@LithpPreth.com

For my wife

Forward

With advances in quantum computer processing, the possibility of mapping entire universes inside computers is now more plausible than ever. While conventional computers rely on the manipulation of bits that can register only one of two values (i.e., 0 or 1), newly constructed quantum computers use quantum bits, or *qubits*, that can register 0, 1, or 0 *and* 1 simultaneously. This quantum property significantly increases processing speed by allowing computers to perform millions of computations in an instant. Seth Lloyd, director of the Center for Extreme Quantum Information Theory at MIT, recently wrote that a quantum computer with a 300-qubit processor could instantaneously perform more calculations than the number of atoms contained in our universe[1]. While there might be a tendency to think that running simulated universes on computers is pure fantasy, at the time of publishing, D-Wave, the current creator of the most advanced quantum computing technology, announced that their team had designed a 512-qubit computer processor. D-Wave also announced a goal of doubling the size of their qubit processing capability once every 12-months[2].

Moore's Law, a 50-year-old computing term attributed to Intel cofounder Gordon Moore, states that the processing power of computers will double every two years. While some have suggested that the end of Moore's law is near due to the constraints dictated by quantum physics and the laws of thermodynamics[3], many scientists are in agreement that with the promise of quantum computers, computational power will begin to grow exponentially proportional to the number of entangled qubits[4]. This expected rapid growth in computer processing is now known as *Rose's Law*, after Geordie Rose, a leader in the field of quantum computing and physics-based processor designs.

If we as humans eventually develop the capability to program and run computer simulated universes, then there is a likelihood that this has already been achieved many times before. Further, there is a high probability that both you and I currently live inside a computer simulation. In this book, I entertain just one central idea, that *you and I exist within a computer simulated universe.* With this one concept I work through a reasonable set of observations, repercussions, predictions and expectations. While I attempt rational and systematic thoughtful discourse, this work is not intended to meet the accepted standards of a philosophic argument. Statements are introduced and conclusions accepted without the traditionally met conditions of necessarily true and unambiguous premises. Having said this, I attempt to follow lines of reasoning to their logical conclusions. My thought is that this book will act as a catalyst for facilitating a deeper logical and fertile dialogue that both expands our thinking on the structure and nature of our universe as well as reconsiders our accepted notions of reality itself.

Computer simulated universes

Human beings exist and at least one universe exists. Our lives are contained within at least one universe and perhaps more than one. Further, our lives exist within one universe and also within zero or greater simulated universes. Whether we exist in just one primary universe or also within a range of simulated universes, the universe we perceive on a day-to-day basis is considered by us to be *real*. That is, we perceive our universe to be guided by reliable physical laws and it appears to be, prima facie, the only universe that exists.

An assumption is made that the universe we find ourselves in has existed for many years (i.e., billions) and is comparably vast. Given this timeframe and expanse, it is probable that a number of intelligent civilizations, in addition to our own, have evolved. At least a very small number of these civilizations have evolved to the extent where complex computer systems have been developed with the capability to run simulated universes that include simulated minds. Even with the existence of a very small number of these advanced civilizations, the frequency of simulated universes that could be run would easily dwarf the number of *primary* or *original* universes that exist (that is to say, one).

With this in mind, there is a high probability that, in addition to a primary or original universe, there should exist within at least one and likely more than one simulated universe.

Given the length of time our primary universe has likely existed since its initial beginning through The Big Bang or some other equivalent, as well as its expansiveness, there is a high probability that a civilization or entity within the primary universe has advanced to the extent of creating a computer generated fully functioning simulated universe. That is to say, there is a high probability that there is at least one simulated universe that exists within our primary universe. Further, these one or more simulated universes have likely existed for a relatively long number of simulated years and are comparably vast. Given this simulated timeframe and simulated expanse, a number of simulated intelligent civilizations have likely evolved. At least a very small number of these simulated civilizations have evolved to the point where simulated complex computers systems have been developed with the ability to run simulated universes. But even with the existence of a very small number of these advanced simulated civilizations, the frequency of simulated universes that could be run by these simulated civilizations would easily dwarf the number of simulated universes that exist within the simulated universe. With this in mind, there is a high probability that, in addition to a primary and at least one simulated universe, inside a simulated universe should exist at least one and likely more than one simulated universe.

Even if just two simulated universes happen to exist directly within our primary universe, then it would follow that there is a higher probability we exist immediately within a simulated universe rather than the *primary* or *original* universe. Also, within the two simulated universes would be a relatively high likelihood that each would contain at least two more simulated universes. Following this logic, there is a higher probability that, rather existing within a simulated universe, we reside within a simulated universe within a simulated universe, and so on, like a series of ever expanding seemingly infinite reflections that appear between two mirrors. Having said this, the number of simulated universes increasing by a factor within simulated universes cannot occur indefinitely. Further, it would be correct to say that the number of simulated universes that exist within simulated universes is not infinite.

The number of simulated universes that can exist within a simulated universe is limited by at least one variable, which is simply the expanse and length of time from the beginning of the primary universe to its present-day moment. With this in mind, it would be correct to say that the moment a primary universe ends would necessarily be the moment all simulated universes that exist within that primary universe also end. It also follows that a discontinuation of any simulated universe that exists between our primary universe and the simulated universe perceived by us to be *real* would necessarily be the moment our *real* universe effectively ends. Additionally, as the number of simulated universes that encompass a particular simulated universe increase, the higher the probability that the particular universe will be more short-lived, even under the assumption of an accelerated and compressed simulated timeframe of a computer simulated universe running inside another simulated universe. As a universe bubble gradually expands, the *universe bubble clusters* contained deep within rapidly become more dense and more quickly expand relative to the outer most universes, before one or more eventually end, or *pop*. The moment an outer universe bubble ruptures is the instant all universes within cease to exist. In sum, no simulated universe can outlast the primary or simulated universe that contains it.

In both simulated and nonsimulated universes, it is difficult to conceptualize how objects are distinct and independent of other objects. Moreover, at the atomic level we know that there are no true boundaries separating one object from another object. With this being said, in a simulated universe the nonindependence of objects might seem more obvious, especially when one is left to consider the presence of something tangible with mass that exists inside something similar to a computer program or system. With the nonindependence of objects as an assumption, nonsimulated and simulated universes are similar in that any nonsimulated object in a nonsimulated universe exists to the extent that any simulated object exists in a simulated universe. Further, both nonsimulated and simulated objects follow predictable cause and effect principles as dictated by the physical properties of their respective nonsimulated and simulated universes. Of note, the nonindependence of objects assumption would also relate to the nonindependence of minds existing within any particular simulation and would argue for the greater likelihood of *global* computer simulated universes running as opposed to *local* simulated universes, as will be discussed later in the book.

In addition to the nonindependence of objects, nonsimulated and simulated universes are also similar in that any two geographical points are separated by what is known as spacetime. Although the nature of spacetime is up for debate, what can be said is that it would be difficult to discuss spacetime in any nonsimulated or simulated universe as being independent of the nonsimulated or simulated objects or matter contained within. At least in a simulated universe, it could be said that any two simulated objects are separated by simulated spacetime, which would then be correct to say that any two simulated objects are not really separated at all. Further, when discussing where any two simulated objects exist in relation to each other, we would merely be using a numerical formula representing something similar to a coordinate system. In this sense, the currently accepted phenomenon of quantum entanglement, that two particles can be intrinsically linked even when located trillions of miles away from each other, would appear to make more intuitive sense. But a more important question is whether any two *non*simulated objects can be truly separated by an intrinsic structure we refer to as spacetime in a *non*simulated universe. If the answer is *no*, then there is a good chance there is fundamentally no real meaningful differences between nonsimulated and simulated universes.

The philosopher Nick Bostrom formed a novel and logically sound argument indicating the distinct possibility that we are living inside a computer simulated universe. In his 2003 article [5], Bostrom wrote that some advanced civilization would likely have developed "enormous computing power". With such a computer system in place, likely a high number of simulations could be run significantly increasing the number of simulated individuals created relative to nonsimulated individuals. This means that there is a higher probability that we ourselves are living in a simulated universe as opposed to a nonsimulated universe. With this in mind, Bostrom argued that at least one of the following must be true: (1) that humans or a species on our technological level are likely to go extinct before reaching a "posthuman" stage; (2) any posthuman civilization is unlikely to run a number of simulations recreating their evolutionary history; (3) we are almost certainly living in a computer simulation. So it goes to follow that if (1) and (2) are both false, then (3) must be accepted. To bridge these statements a different manner, it could be said that unless we happen to be currently residing in a simulated universe, then our descendants either will become extinct prior to developing the ability to run computer simulations recreating our evolutionary history or will not have much of an interest to run them. One of the basic assumptions at the core of this argument is something known as *substrate independence*, which is the notion that conscious minds can be created using the substrate of silicon-based computers (or something similar) in addition to the substrate of carbon-based biological neurons from which our own consciousness emerges. Of course, when discussing the notion of simulations running within simulations, there would appear to be much less relevance considering whether conscious minds are truly dependent on elemental structures that possess mass, such as carbon versus silicon.

If computer simulated universes exist, then it is likely that a proportion of these simulated universes have been designed to resemble close copies of the universe that contains the simulation. As the number of simulated universes contained within simulated universes increase, the higher the number of these copies of copies should exist. With this in mind, one possible means to discover whether we reside within a simulated universe would be to identify these repeating patterns indicating the specific number of simulated universes that bridge us to our primary universe.

An analogy would be an LP record of recorded live music that has been remastered into a digital CD. As audiophiles may tell you, information is lost when analog produced sound waves are transformed to sound waves created by digital *sampling*. Typically, even additional digital data is lost over each successive CD copy. However, with each copy typically enough data is retained to realize the purpose of the created CD, to accurately produce the simulated sound waves that closely represent the sound waves created by the original music. This leads to an interesting possibility. When analyzing any given CD copy, one could, theoretically, be able to devise an analytical method for counting the number of CD copies of copies created since the original recording. The same could be true with devising a method for counting the number of simulated universes that exist within simulated universes.

Why run computer simulated universes?

If we assume that we reside within at least one computer simulated universe, then what are the primary reasons for running simulations? Some possibilities are as follows:

1. Simulations are running forward and in compressed time to gain knowledge of some future condition or future possible outcome.
2. Simulations are running backward and in compressed time to gain knowledge of some earlier condition or antecedents to later states of the universe.
3. Simulations are running forward, concurrently in time, and yoked to another universe to gain knowledge of some present or persisting condition. A present or persisting condition could be an increasing threat where implementing yoked computer simulations could compare various proposed solutions, such as hypothetical fixes to combat adverse global climate change or rapid population growth threatening an advanced civilization. As these solutions slowly emerge, innovations and modifications would then be introduced into the *real* universe.
4. Simulations are running to discern whether the reality experienced by an advanced

civilization or entity happens to exist within one or more simulations.

5. An advanced civilization develops simulations that are basically so simple to run that they merely represent a natural progression of something comparable to simple computer programming, automated computer systems, or computer gaming. If this were true, the entity running the simulation would almost certainly realize that it itself was functioning within a simulation or series of simulations.

In such cases, it would be correct to say that the aggregate of our combined lives, along with the physical structure of the universe around us, is merely the necessary variables, factors, or means to an end created to calculate one or more possible outcomes for the advanced civilization or entity running the simulation. Of course, the advanced civilization or entity running the simulation would likely be subject to the same treatment itself, as the necessary variables, factors, or means to an end created to discern one or more possible outcomes. From a pseudo-evolutionary perspective, the consequence of running computer simulated universes, over a long period of time, should be the increased long-term survival for those civilizations when compared to advanced civilizations who do not or cannot run them. In conclusion, it could be accurately stated that one purpose of our lives, when taken in total, is to generate possible solutions to obstacles and problems, as defined by the entity or advanced civilization on the next level up running the simulation.

If an advanced civilization develops the capacity to run one simulation then, within a relatively short period of time, that same civilization should be able to run a multitude of simulations concurrently. If the goal for a proportion of these simulations is to further advance the civilization and its ability to learn something about itself over a relatively short simulated timeframe, then intrinsic to each active simulation would be some fundamental limitations, including the simulations' civilizations' proclivity to destroy themselves or be destroyed by other agents prior to the point of either advancing to the technological equivalent of the civilization running the simulation or reaching the capacity to run simulated universes themselves. However, by the sheer running of a multitude of simulations, the probability would increase that simulated civilizations would be created that would advance far enough to either become the technological equivalent of the civilization running the simulation or to create their own simulated civilizations. It follows that at some point a simulated civilization would be created that, within an accelerated and compressed time frame, evolves even further than the advanced civilization running the simulation. In such a case, the amount of important information that could be obtained by the advanced civilization running the simulation would be immeasurable. It is staggering to think how quickly our species might gain important knowledge and evolve once we arrive to the point of running universe simulations that run universe simulations, and so on. If Artificial Intelligence (AI) is defined as the appearance of complex computer programs capable of performing difficult cognitive tasks[6], then we might be describing AI in its most authentic and undeniable sense.

The artificial and natural selection of simulated universes

Artificial Selection is a process in the breeding of animals and cultivation of plants by which the breeder or cultivator chooses to perpetuate only those forms having certain desirable characteristics [7] . Assuming that simulated universes do exist, this process would represent a reasonable framework for explaining how universe characteristics happen to evolve over time. Although the problem with *intentionality* will be addressed later, a civilization or entity would be said to intentionally choose certain physical properties that are considered desirable, based on previously run simulations, and systematically favor those traits to be included in future simulations. It is this so-called intentional reproduction of a population of simulated universes with desirable traits that would appear to be a good fit when considering why particular types of simulated universes might appear and flourish more than others. Of importance, the process of artificial selection often involves the appearance of unintended physical traits that are closely aligned with the sought after traits. Consequently, if we look closely at our own universe, we might expect to see a range of necessary or obvious *defects* that happen to exist because the favorable traits that have been selected for also exist.

Natural Selection is the process by which organisms having traits that better enable them to adapt to specific environmental pressures will tend to survive and reproduce in greater numbers than others of their kind, thus ensuring the perpetuation of those favorable traits in succeeding generations[8]. The process of natural selection does an excellent job explaining the fitness and long-term survival of all species on our planet, including human beings. Although the process of artificial selection would appear to perform a sufficient job explaining the appearance of certain physical traits in simulated universes, a process similar to natural selection could be at work as well when attempting to explain the general evolution of simulated universes over time.

With a multitude of simulated universes running, there would be a variation of simulated physical properties from universe to universe. It is unclear whether something analogous to *random mutations* would occur, but simulated universes with certain variants or physical traits would tend to survive longer and produce more hospitable environments that would, in turn, produce a higher number of simulated universes with an increased amount of those variants or physical traits relative to other simulated universes. So, over time, there would be a tendency for simulated civilizations to reside in more and more hospitable and longer-lived simulated universes until any number of catastrophes unfold, such as the sudden end of a planetary system in one simulated universe that happens to be running another simulated universe. An interesting potential consequence of this process would be the appearance and branching out of different species of simulated universes that would show little resemblance to each other and with each possessing wildly different properties of matter and energy.

One distinction that is often made between artificial and natural selection is the notion that artificial selection involves *intentionality* (by the agent making the selection) while natural selection does not. But, as we will see later in this book, this idea is thought to be a distinction without a difference. That is to say, there is fundamentally no room for intentional states or motives when considering both nonsimulated and simulated universes.

A favored current response to the question why our universe seems to be constructed with almost perfect physical properties to support life, is that we happen to live in a universe with almost perfect physical properties to support life, and therefore happen to be around to ask that particular question. However, an alternative explanation is that universes, over time, have been selected for particular physical properties, with an end result of creating more and more habitable, hospitable and longer-lived universes. Yes, the laws of physics might actually evolve.

The computer simulated universes running now are either more locally or globally focused

There are an infinite number of possible computer simulated universes that could run at any given time. Each active simulation could be described as either being more locally or globally focused. A running local simulation would indicate that the universe was created with the more narrow focus of taking on the unique perspective of our region of the universe, our galaxy, our planetary system, our civilization, a selection of individuals, or even one particular individual within our civilization. A local simulation might be designed to help address more specific concerns, such as a later simulation of me attempting to examine my original self that existed some time before. Having said this, it would appear logical that a mind existing within a simulation would not be able to interact realistically and fully with other minds unless those other minds were as fully developed and interconnected as the mind in the simulation. The possibility that minds, in addition to other objects, are not able to exist or function independently in a simulation would decrease the feasibility and likelihood of running more local simulations and increase the probability of running larger full universe computer simulations.

If we do happen to reside in a more global universe simulation, we would expect to find a general uniformity of detail, types, and the amount of information that exists across the universe, independent of how far away we are able to peer or travel in spacetime. Regardless of whether more local or global simulations are running, it is conjectured that there would be active computer programs functioning across a range of concurrently running or completed simulations for the purpose of analyzing important key data through complex meta-analyses.

The computer simulated universes running now do not necessarily have the same beginning point, ending point, or even directionality

Prima facie, it would appear that most simulated universes should have relatively the same beginning point (i.e., The Big Bang) and ending point (i.e., something akin to The Big Rip, or the uniform disintegration of all matter and energy into radiation and unbound elementary particles). However, depending on which questions are being asked, this would not necessarily be the case and that any particular computer simulated universe might have only needed to have begun partially through its lifecycle. Further, if we happened to reside in such a universe, then our past histories would merely be part of the designated starting point of the universe and our past memories merely our physical brain states that would happen to exist as the program running our simulated universe was launched.

The *feel* of time, at least from a human perspective with our manner of forming memories, is something that runs in only one particular direction, forward. However, the physics in which we are accustomed (entropy aside) does not appear to make much of a distinction regarding time running forward as opposed to time running backward. Although masked by our own unique point of view, the simulation we happen to find ourselves in could just as easily be running backward for the purpose of understanding some earlier condition or antecedents essential to later states of the universe.

Simulation divergence

Any particular simulation could be programmed to diverge into two or more simulations at specific time/space points or at any predetermined decision point. This could occur for a number of different reasons, such as for the purpose of manipulating one particular variable in a manner that would, in turn, generate two or more competing solutions to a given presenting problem. In such cases, near parallel universes would immediately be created that would theoretically, over time, branch further and further away from each other in appearance and other physical attributes.

There is an indistinguishable influence between the computer simulated universes we might create and the entity or civilization that runs our own simulation

Computer programs are often written that contain subroutines, which are just a series of instructions contained within programs to perform certain tasks when specific conditions are met. After subroutines run, typically, they are looped back to the general computer program, which will then run the same or differently depending on the information that was returned to the program. Although a computer program could be said to be in control of its subroutines by executing the codes that activate them and under what circumstances, subroutines could be said to be in control of a computer program by changing the manner of how it runs depending on the subroutines' outputs.

With this in mind, the causal relationships between simulated universes and the simulated universes contained within would work both ways. On the face of it, it might appear that an advanced civilization or entity has complete control over any particular simulated universe that it is running. However, the outcome of any particular running simulated universe would necessarily alter the fundamental physical attributes of the advanced civilization or entity running the simulation, and thereby change, even if in some minor way, its future course.

In sum, when considering the possibility of computer programs running universe simulations, it becomes readily apparent that everything is truly interconnected in our universe, and even across universes. There is no independent self, or universe for that matter, that could occur outside of a system. And there are no independent actors inside of a computer program.

Computer programs do not have free will

Any object functioning within the physical laws of any particular universe does not have free will. This includes computer systems, human beings, planets and chairs. Regarding human beings, every engaged in behavior or experienced thought cannot appear out of thin air. Behavior and cognition *must* be the result of prior causes because our brains obey the same laws of a cause and effect physical universe like any other physical object. Despite the fact that having free will is a conspicuous logical impossibility, this delusion persists across cultures. For more thorough philosophical and scientific arguments on the matter, there happens to be a wide range of thought-provoking literature to peruse.[9,10]

More interesting than the notion of free will are the implications of what an absence of free will has on the notion of self. Regardless of whether we reside in a computer simulated universe, I am a highly complex feedback control system with my behavioral outputs being entirely explained by the total sum and configuration of inputs. And you are this way too. If we are both undergoing these processes at the same time, then your thoughts and behaviors change me (in a fundamental neurobiological sense) as much as my thoughts and behaviors change myself. With this realization, the distinction I make between you and me is largely artificial. And even though the neurons in our brains are not directly connected to each other, they might as well be. This is because sensory information exchanged back and forth between you and me inescapably make us both part of the same process. It follows that if the difference between you and me is predominately because your brain is in your head and my brain is in my head, this now appears to be a distinction without much of a difference. In fact, because you and I do not act separately from each other, distinguishing you and me at the individual/person level can actually seem sort of arbitrary.

The notion of simulated universes makes all too clear the absence of free will. We never think of a computer program or computer system as having free will, or the ability to make independent *choices* or engage in independent *decision-making*. On the contrary, the outputs of a computer program are entirely dependent on the physical laws of the universe running the program as well as how the programming code was written to indicate which actions would be performed when which conditions were met.

Within any given universe, there is a set of physical laws governing a computer system contained within and how that computer system functions, even if that computer system happens to run a highly complex computer program, such as a simulated universe. Further, any output generated by a simulated universe would be subject to the physical laws of the universe running the simulated universe along with the manner the program code has been created to run the simulated universe. A computer program designed to simulate a universe could be written to run an entirely new and different set of physical laws and the manner in which that simulated universe behaves would be subject to those laws. However, in another sense, it would also be subject to the laws of the simulated universe that is running the simulated universe.

It is important to note that we have been discussing simulated universes in the sense that advanced civilizations are required to create and then run them. While this might seem true on the surface, it is more useful to view the appearance of advanced civilizations as just one particular condition to be met before one running simulated universe can create and run another simulated universe. Further, with the absence of free will there is no longer a meaningful distinction between an individual or group of individuals *deciding* to run a simulated universe versus one simulated universe *deciding* to run another simulated universe. The simulated universe and the individuals contained within are all intrinsically part of the same complex system.

On artificial intelligence

If computer simulated universes happen to exist, then there is a high probability that we reside within at least one and likely more than one simulated universe. If this is the case, then the question of whether we as humans might someday develop artificial intelligence (AI) suddenly becomes a moot point. That is, if we as humans reside within a computer simulated universe, then our existence is intrinsically linked to the activity of a computer program that has generated the conditions allowing our brains to have evolved and existed, *artificially.* This means that our species has evolved inside a computer program, a massless universe lacking a formal structure we have come to know and accept as spacetime. We have been searching for AI but maybe the technological singularity, or the emergence of a high–tech superintelligence, has already come and gone. We have known a computer all along with the capacity to run fully functional AI programs. And it happens to be the very same computer that is currently running our simulated universe inclusive of our simulated minds.

The presence of simulated universes gets us no closer (or further) to god or a true master creator

When considering the notion of us living within a simulated universe, it is possible to say that there could be a tangible designer, maybe a creator or some individual who could be referred to as *God*, who may or may not be omnipotent, omniscient, or both during the duration of the computer simulation. Of course, when considering the notion of a one true God as typically defined by our western tradition as a master creator of everything, this still leads us to an unresolvable logical fallacy. Further, it begs the question that if, in fact, our simulated universe has a designer, then who designed the designer's universe, who designed the designer's designer's universe, and so on? Since an infinite regress of explanations is not possible, we are left with being no closer (or further) from one true master creator of everything.

As previously discussed, when considering the implications of living within a simulated universe, a distinct possibility is raised that our own universe was created by a later, more advanced rendition of ourselves. With this in mind, it could be said that our future selves are the creators or *Gods*, if you like, to our present day selves.   Which is to say, that when we attempt to look to God for his purpose and plan for our lives, we might be quite literally looking into ourselves.

The ethics of running simulated universes

Borrowing from the animal welfare model, one could argue that the greater the capacity for sentience and self-awareness in a species, the greater is its moral worth. In our own civilization, we know that there can be a wide range of cognitive abilities across animal species and it would seem difficult to argue that humans and all animals on Earth have equal moral worth. A *sliding scale* position regarding the moral status of animals states that there is a spectrum of moral worth among animals where humans are thought to be at the top. The sliding scale position is generally believed to be a reasonable manner to consider these issues and suggests that although all animals have some moral worth, humans' unique capacity for rationality, self-awareness and emotional suffering raises our moral worth above other species[11].

If we are residing within a computer simulated universe, then the advanced civilization or entity running our universe would presumably have a greater capacity for rationality, self-awareness and emotional suffering than our own. But a key question here would be *how much more* capacity for sentience and self-awareness could individuals in an advanced civilization possess relative to human beings, as we know them? If an appropriate analogy turns out to be individuals in an advanced civilization are to human beings as human beings are to chimpanzees, then individuals living in the advanced civilization would have a moral responsibility to treat us humanely without purposefully creating a painful universe, not prematurely ending our universe, and allowing either our lives to naturally play themselves out or our universe to naturally end after a vast majority of the star-making gas has been effectively exhausted.

If, on the other hand, an appropriate analogy turns out to be individuals in an advanced civilization are to human beings as human beings are to oysters, then individuals living in the advanced civilization might not internalize any real moral responsibility for our civilization's well being. Presumably, just the mere emergence of the self-knowledge that we are living within a simulated universe and that our universe could prematurely end at any time would increase the moral responsibility that an advanced civilization might experience toward us.

Of course, the concern regarding living in a simulated universe that might prematurely end is a concern based under the assumption that it would take a relatively long time to run any given simulated universe from beginning to end. If, in fact, simulated universes could be run in an instant, then the worry regarding simulated universes prematurely ending would generally become a nonissue. However, the moral responsibility of agents creating universes that are *pain free* as possible would likely continue.

Achieving immortality

If we do happen to exist inside a computer simulation, then we are no longer necessarily mortal. Presumably, an advanced civilization running a simulated universe would also have the capacity to manipulate any of the generated data upon the simulation's conclusion in almost any manner it saw fit. This would include the ability to rerun the same simulation or capture chunks of information from a completed simulation to be used within a newly constructed simulation for further development. An advanced civilization running our simulated universe would have the ability to extend our lives indefinitely, or at least up until the point when any particular simulated universe that contains our simulated universe effectively ends. It is thought that a computer system with the complexity to run universe simulations would also have the complexity to transfer our histories, memories and sense of self-awareness from simulation to simulation. This might be the closest we will ever get to something similar to an afterlife.

An advanced civilization running a simulated universe, presumably, would be able to run simulations recreating or closely replicating its evolutionary history. It follows that a proportion of these simulations are also contained within the evolutionary history simulations of other advanced civilizations running their own evolutionary history simulations, and so on. Though potentially not a preferred outcome, in a sense, we as humans might have already achieved immortality by living the same or similar lives over and over. So quite possibly, whenever we eat, go to work, or take out the garbage, you and I are just one reflection in the middle of a series of ever expanding, seemingly infinite reflections. Or maybe even a better analogy is that you and I are locked somewhere inside a vast set of Russian wooden dolls, with one or more dolls each nested inside another and another and another. A *Matryoshkaverse*.

Closing thoughts

My intent was that this book would act as a catalyst for forming a broader creative and logical dialogue that both reconsiders and expands our accepted thinking on the nature of our universe and reality itself. Here are some final thoughts to consider:

1. You now possess the self-knowledge that you quite possibly reside within a computer simulated universe.
2. It is plausible that some local simulations are currently running that are selecting for the discovery of the initial emergence of this self-knowledge.
3. The plausibility of these *discovery simulations* as well as this new self-knowledge further increases the likelihood that you exist within a computer simulation, and that the particular simulation that you find yourself is closely associated with the initial emergence of this knowledge.

A NOTE ABOUT THE AUTHOR

Mark J. Solomon is a neuropsychologist who resides with his wife, Jennifer, in North Carolina. He received a Bachelor's degree from Washington University in St. Louis and a Ph.D. from Texas Tech University with an internship at Tulane University Medical Center and a post-doctoral fellowship at Brown University. In addition to a neuropsychologist, Dr. Solomon happens to be the fine wine director for a major auction house. He can be contacted through his publisher at *Editor@LithpPreth.com*.

[1] Lloyd, S., Mohseni, M., & Rebentrost, P. (2013). Quantum algorithms for supervised and unsupervised machine learning. *Journal article submitted for review.*

[2] D-Wave. (2013). D-Wave Two™ Quantum Computer Selected for New Quantum Artificial Intelligence Initiative, System to be Installed at NASA's Ames Research Center, and Operational in Q3. [Press release]. Retrieved from http://www.dwavesys.com/en/pressreleases.html

[3] Paul, Ian (2013). The end of moore's law is on the horizon. *PCWorld*, April 3rd.

[4] Metz, Cade (2013). Google's quantum computer proven to be real thing (almost). *Wired*, June.

[5] Bostrom, Nick (2003). Are you living in a computer simulation? *Philosophical Quarterly, 53*, 243-255.

[6] Eysenck, Michael (1990), "Artificial Intelligence," in M.W. Eysenck (ed.), *The Blackwell Dictionary of Cognitive Psychology* (Oxford: Basil Blackwell): 22.

[7] Artificial Selection [Def. 1]. (n.d.). *Dictionary Reference Online.* In Random House. Retrieved August 4, 2013, from http://www.dictionary.reference.com/browse/artificial+selection

[8] Natural Selection [Def. 1]. *Dictionary Reference Online.* In Random House. Retrieved August 4, 2013, from http://www.dictionary.reference.com/browse/natural+selection

[9] Harris, Sam (2012). *Free will.* New York, NY: Free Press.

[10] Wegner, Daniel (2003). *The illusion of conscious will.* Cambridge: A Bradford Book.

[11] Fieser, James (2008). *Moral issues that divide us.* Book in progress.

www.ingramcontent.com/pod-product-compliance
Lightning Source LLC
Chambersburg PA
CBHW060928050326
40689CB00013B/3008